THE LAW

THE LAW

BY

FREDERIC BASTIAT

ISBN: 978-93-5128-986-9(PB)

First Published in 1850
Indian Reprint in 2017

Published by

Kalpaz Publications
C-30, Satyawati Nagar,
Delhi – 110052
E-mail: kalpaz@hotmail.com
Website: kalpazpublications.com
Ph.: +91-9212142040

Foreword

Anyone building a personal library of liberty must include in it a copy of Frédéric Bastiat's classic essay, "The Law." First published in 1850 by the great French economist and journalist, it is as clear a statement as has ever been made of the original American ideal of government, as proclaimed in the Declaration of Independence, that the main purpose of any government is the protection of the lives, liberties, and property of its citizens.

Bastiat believed that all human beings possessed the God-given, natural rights of "individuality, liberty, property." "This is man," he wrote. These "three gifts from God precede all human legislation." But even in his time—writing in the late 1840s—Bastiat was alarmed over how the law had been "perverted" into an instrument of what he called legal plunder. Far from protecting individual rights, the law was increasingly used to deprive one group of citizens of those rights for the benefit of another group, and especially for the benefit of the state itself. He condemned the legal plunder of protectionist tariffs, government subsidies of all kinds, progressive taxation, public schools, government "jobs" programs, minimum wage laws, welfare, usury laws, and more.

Bastiat's warnings of the dire effects of legal plunder are as relevant today as they were the day he first issued them. The system of legal plunder (which many now celebrate as "democracy") will erase from everyone's conscience, he wrote, the distinction between justice and injustice. The plundered classes will eventually figure out how to enter the political game and plunder their fellow man. Legislation will never be guided by any principles of justice, but only by brute political force.

The great French champion of liberty also forecast the corruption of education by the state. Those who held "government-endowed teaching positions," he wrote, would rarely criticize legal plunder lest their government endowments be ended.

The system of legal plunder would also greatly exaggerate the importance of politics in society. That would be a most unhealthy development as it would encourage even more citizens to seek to improve their own well-being not by producing goods and services for the marketplace but by plundering their fellow citizens through politics.

Bastiat was also wise enough to anticipate what modern economists call "rent seeking" and "rent avoidance" behavior. These two clumsy phrases refer, respectively, to the phenomena of lobbying for political favors (legal plunder), and of engaging in political activity directed at protecting oneself from being the victim of plunder seekers. (For example, the steel manufacturing industry lobbies for high tariffs on steel, whereas steel-using industries, like the automobile industry, can be expected to lobby against high tariffs on steel).

The reason why modern economists are concerned about "rent seeking" is the opportunity cost involved: the more time, effort and money that is spent by businesses on conniving to manipulate politics—merely transferring wealth—the less time is spent on producing goods and services, which increases wealth. Thus, legal plunder impoverishes the entire society despite the fact that a small (but politically influential) part of the society benefits from it.

It is remarkable, in reading "The Law," how perfectly accurate Bastiat was in describing the statists of his day which, it turns out, were not much different from the statists of today or any other day. The French "socialists" of Bastiat's day espoused doctrines that perverted charity, education, and morals, for one thing. True charity does not begin with the robbery of taxation, he pointed out. Government schooling is inevitably an exercise in statist brainwashing, not genuine education; and it is hardly "moral" for a large gang (government) to (legally) rob one segment of the population, keep most of the loot, and share a little of it with various "needy" individuals.

Socialists want "to play God," Bastiat observed, anticipating all the future tyrants and despots of the world who would try to remake the world in their image, whether that image would be communism, fascism, the "glorious union," or "global democracy." Bastiat also observed that socialists wanted forced conformity; rigid regimentation of the population through pervasive regulation; forced equality of wealth; and dictatorship. As such, they were the mortal enemies of liberty.

"Dictatorship" need not involve an actual dictator. All that was needed, said Bastiat, was "the laws," enacted by a Congress or a Parliament, that would achieve the same effect: forced conformity.

Bastiat was also wise to point out that the world has far too many "great men," "fathers of their countries," etc., who in reality are usually nothing but petty tyrants with a sick and compulsive desire to rule over others. The defenders of the free society should have a healthy disrespect for all such men.

Bastiat admired America and pointed to the America of 1850 as being as close as any society in the world to his ideal of a government that protected individual rights to life, liberty, and property. There were two major exeptions, however: the twin evils of slavery and protectionist tariffs.

Frédéric Bastiat died on Christmas Eve, 1850, and did not live to observe the convulsions that the America he admired so much would go through in the next fifteen years (and longer). It is unlikely that he would have considered the U.S. government's military invasion of the Southern states in 1861, the killing of some 300,000 citizens, and the bombing, burning, and plundering of the region's cities, towns, farms, and businesses as being consistent in any way with the protection of the lives, liberties and properties of those citizens as promised by the Declaration of Independence. Had he lived to see all of this, he most likely would have added "legal murder" to "legal plunder" as one of the two great sins of government. He would likely have viewed the post-war Republican Party, with its 50 percent average tariff rates, its massive corporate welfare schemes, and its 25-year campaign of genocide against the Plains Indians as first-rate plunderers and traitors to the American ideal.

In the latter pages of "The Law" Bastiat offers the sage advice that what was really needed was "a science of economics" that would explain the harmony (or lack thereof) of a free society (as opposed to socialism). He made a major contribution to this end himself with the publication of his book, *Economic Harmonies*, which can be construed as a precursor to the modern literature of the Austrian School of economics. There is no substitute for a solid understanding of the market order (and of the realities of politics) when it comes to combating the kinds of destructive socialistic schemes that plagued Bastiat's day as well as ours. Anyone who reads this great essay along with other free-market classics, such as Henry Hazlitt's *Economics in One Lesson* and Murray Rothbard's *Power and Market*, will possess enough intellectual ammunition to debunk the socialist fantasies of this or any other day.

Thomas J. DiLorenzo
May 2007

Thomas DiLorenzo is professor of economics at Loyola College in Maryland and a member of the senior faculty of the Mises Institute.

THE LAW[1]

The law perverted! The law—and, in its wake, all the collective forces of the nation—the law, I say, not only diverted from its proper direction, but made to pursue one entirely contrary! The law become the tool of every kind of avarice, instead of being its check! The law guilty of that very iniquity which it was its mission to punish! Truly, this is a serious fact, if it exists, and one to which I feel bound to call the attention of my fellow citizens.

We hold from God the gift that, as far as we are concerned, contains all others, Life—physical, intellectual, and moral life.

But life cannot support itself. He who has bestowed it, has entrusted us with the care of supporting it, of developing it, and of perfecting it. To that end, He has provided us with a collection of wonderful faculties; He has plunged us into the midst of a variety of elements. It is by

---

[1]First published in 1850.

the application of our faculties to these elements that the phenomena of assimilation and of appropriation, by which life pursues the circle that has been assigned to it are realized.

Existence, faculties, assimilation—in other words, personality, liberty, property—this is man.

It is of these three things that it may be said, apart from all demagogic subtlety, that they are anterior and superior to all human legislation.

It is not because men have made laws, that personality, liberty, and property exist. On the contrary, it is because personality, liberty, and property exist beforehand, that men make laws. What, then, is law? As I have said elsewhere, it is the collective organization of the individual right to lawful defense.

Nature, or rather God, has bestowed upon every one of us the right to defend his person, his liberty, and his property, since these are the three constituent or preserving elements of life; elements, each of which is rendered complete by the others, and that cannot be understood without them. For what are our faculties, but the extension of our personality? and what is property, but an extension of our faculties?

If every man has the right of defending, even by force, his person, his liberty, and his property, a number of men have the right to combine together to extend, to organize a common force to provide regularly for this defense.

Collective right, then, has its principle, its reason for existing, its lawfulness, in individual right; and the common force cannot rationally have any other end, or any other mission, than that of the isolated forces for which it is substituted. Thus, as the force of an individual cannot lawfully touch the person, the liberty, or the property of another individual—for the same reason, the common force cannot lawfully be used to destroy the person, the liberty, or the property of individuals or of classes.

For this perversion of force would be, in one case as in the other, in contradiction to our premises. For who will dare to say that force has been given to us, not to defend our rights, but to annihilate the equal rights of our brethren? And if this be not true of every individual force, acting independently, how can it be true of the collective force, which is only the organized union of isolated forces?

Nothing, therefore, can be more evident than this: The law is the organization of the natural right of lawful defense; it is the substitution of collective for individual forces, for the purpose of acting in the sphere in which they have a right to act, of doing what they have a right to do, to secure persons, liberties, and properties, and to maintain each in its right, so as to cause justice to reign over all.

And if a people established upon this basis were to exist, it seems to me that order would prevail among them in their acts as well as in their ideas. It seems to me that such a people would have the most simple, the most economical, the least oppressive, the least to be felt, the most restrained, the most just, and, consequently, the most stable Government that could be imagined, whatever its political form might be.

For under such an administration, everyone would feel that he possessed all the fullness, as well as all the responsibility of his existence. So long as personal safety was ensured, so long as labor was free, and the fruits of labor secured against all unjust attacks, no one would have any difficulties to contend with in the State. When prosperous, we should not, it is true, have to thank the State for our success; but when unfortunate, we should no more think of taxing it with our disasters than our peasants think of attributing to it the arrival of hail or of frost. We should know it only by the inestimable blessing of Safety.

It may further be affirmed, that, thanks to the non-intervention of the State in private affairs, our wants and their satisfactions would develop themselves in their natural order. We should not see poor families seeking for literary instruction before they were supplied with bread. We should not see towns peopled at the expense of rural districts, nor rural districts at the expense of towns. We should not see those great displacements of capital, of labor, and of population, that legislative measures occasion; displacements that render so uncertain and precarious the very sources of existence, and thus enlarge to such an extent the responsibility of Governments.

Unhappily, law is by no means confined to its own sphere. Nor is it merely in some ambiguous and debatable views that it has left its proper sphere. It has done more than this. It has acted in direct opposition to its proper end; it has destroyed its own object; it has been employed in annihilating that justice which it ought to have established, in effacing amongst Rights, that limit which it was its true mission to respect; it has placed the collective force in the service of those who wish to traffic, without risk and without scruple, in the persons, the liberty, and the property of others; it has converted plunder into a right, that it may protect it, and lawful defense into a crime, that it may punish it.

How has this perversion of law been accomplished? And what has resulted from it?

The law has been perverted through the influence of two very different causes—naked greed and misconceived philanthropy.

Let us speak of the former. Self-preservation and development is the common aspiration of all men, in such a way that if every one enjoyed the free exercise of his faculties and the free disposition of their fruits, social progress would be incessant, uninterrupted, inevitable.

But there is also another disposition which is common to them. This is to live and to develop, when they can, at the expense of one another. This is no rash imputation, emanating from a gloomy, uncharitable spirit. History bears witness to the truth of it, by the incessant wars, the migrations of races, sectarian oppressions, the universality of slavery, the frauds in trade, and the monopolies with which its annals abound. This fatal disposition has its origin in the very constitution of man—in that primitive, and universal, and invincible sentiment that urges it towards its well-being, and makes it seek to escape pain.

Man can only derive life and enjoyment from a perpetual search and appropriation; that is, from a perpetual application of his faculties to objects, or from labor. This is the origin of property.

But also he may live and enjoy, by seizing and appropriating the productions of the faculties of his fellow men. This is the origin of plunder.

Now, labor being in itself a pain, and man being naturally inclined to avoid pain, it follows, and history proves it, that wherever plunder is less burdensome than labor, it prevails; and neither religion nor morality can, in this case, prevent it from prevailing.

When does plunder cease, then? When it becomes more burdensome and more dangerous than labor. It is very evident that the proper aim of law is to oppose the fatal tendency to plunder with the powerful obstacle of collective force; that all its measures should be in favor of property, and against plunder.

But the law is made, generally, by one man, or by one class of men. And as law cannot exist without the sanction and the support of a preponderant force, it must finally place this force in the hands of those who legislate.

This inevitable phenomenon, combined with the fatal tendency that, we have said, exists in the heart of man, explains the almost universal perversion of law. It is easy to conceive that, instead of being a check upon injustice, it becomes its most invincible instrument.

It is easy to conceive that, according to the power of the legislator, it destroys for its own profit, and in different degrees amongst the rest of the community, personal independence by slavery, liberty by oppression, and property by plunder.

It is in the nature of men to rise against the injustice of which they are the victims. When, therefore, plunder is organized by law, for the profit of those who perpetrate it, all the plundered classes tend, either by peaceful or revolutionary means, to enter in some way into the manufacturing of laws. These classes, according to the degree of enlightenment at which they have arrived, may propose to themselves two very different ends, when they thus attempt the attainment of their political rights; either they may wish to put an end to lawful plunder, or they may desire to take part in it.

Woe to the nation where this latter thought prevails amongst the masses, at the moment when they, in their turn, seize upon the legislative power!

Up to that time, lawful plunder has been exercised by the few upon the many, as is the case in countries where the right of legislating is confined to a few hands. But now it has become universal, and the equilibrium is sought in universal plunder. The injustice that society contains, instead of being rooted out of it, is generalized. As soon as the injured classes have recovered their political rights, their first thought is not to abolish plunder (this would suppose them to possess enlightenment, which they cannot have), but to organize against the other classes, and to their own detriment, a system of reprisals—as if it was necessary, before the reign of justice arrives, that all should undergo a cruel retribution—some for their iniquity and some for their ignorance.

It would be impossible, therefore, to introduce into society a greater change and a greater evil than this—the conversion of the law into an instrument of plunder.

What would be the consequences of such a perversion? It would require volumes to describe them all. We must content ourselves with pointing out the most striking.

In the first place, it would efface from everybody's conscience the distinction between justice and injustice. No society can exist unless the laws are respected to a certain degree, but the safest way to make them respected is to make them respectable. When law and morality are in contradiction to each other, the citizen finds himself in the cruel alternative of either losing his moral sense, or of losing his respect for the law—two evils of equal magnitude, between which it would be difficult to choose.

It is so much in the nature of law to support justice that in the minds of the masses they are one and the same. There is in all of us a strong disposition to regard what is lawful as legitimate, so much so that many falsely derive all justice from law. It is sufficient, then, for the law to order and sanction plunder, that it may appear to many consciences just and sacred. Slavery, protection, and monopoly find defenders, not only in those who profit by them, but in those who suffer by them. If you suggest a doubt as to the morality of these institutions, it is said directly—"You are a dangerous experimenter, a utopian, a theorist, a despiser of the laws; you would shake the basis upon which society rests."

If you lecture upon morality, or political economy, official bodies will be found to make this request to the Government:

> That henceforth science be taught not only with sole reference to free exchange (to liberty, property, and justice), as has been the case up to the present time, but also, and especially, with reference to the facts and legislation (contrary to liberty, property, and justice) that regulate French industry.
>
> That, in public lecterns salaried by the treasury, the professor abstain rigorously from endangering in the slightest degree the respect due to the laws now in force.[2]

So that if a law exists that sanctions slavery or monopoly, oppression or plunder, in any form whatever, it must not even be mentioned—for how can it be mentioned without damaging the respect that it inspires? Still further, morality and political economy must be taught in connection with this law—that is, under the supposition that it must be just, only because it is law.

---

[2]General Council of Manufactures, Agriculture, and Commerce, 6th of May, 1850.

Another effect of this deplorable perversion of the law is that it gives to human passions and to political struggles, and, in general, to politics, properly so called, an exaggerated importance.

I could prove this assertion in a thousand ways. But I shall confine myself, by way of an illustration, to bringing it to bear upon a subject which has of late occupied everybody's mind: universal suffrage.

Whatever may be thought of it by the adepts of the school of Rousseau, which professes to be very far advanced, but which I consider 20 centuries behind, universal suffrage (taking the word in its strictest sense) is not one of those sacred dogmas with respect to which examination and doubt are crimes.

Serious objections may be made to it.

In the first place, the word universal conceals a gross sophism. There are, in France, 36,000,000 inhabitants. To make the right of suffrage universal, 36,000,000 electors should be reckoned. The most extended system reckons only 9,000,000. Three persons out of four, then, are excluded; and more than this, they are excluded by the fourth. Upon what principle is this exclusion founded? Upon the principle of incapacity. Universal suffrage, then, means: universal suffrage of those who are capable. In point of fact, who are the capable? Are age, sex, and judicial condemnations the only conditions to which incapacity is to be attached?

On taking a nearer view of the subject, we may soon perceive the reason why the right of suffrage depends upon the presumption of incapacity; the most extended system differing from the most restricted in the conditions on which this incapacity depends, and which constitutes not a difference in principle, but in degree.

This motive is, that the elector does not stipulate for himself, but for everybody.

If, as the republicans of the Greek and Roman tone pretend, the right of suffrage had fallen to the lot of every one at his birth, it would be an injustice to adults to prevent women and children from voting. Why are they prevented? Because they are presumed to be incapable. And why is incapacity a reason for exclusion? Because the elector does not reap alone the responsibility of his vote; because every vote engages and affects the community at large; because the community has a right to demand some assurances, as regards the acts upon which its well-being and its existence depend.

I know what might be said in answer to this. I know what might be objected. But this is not the place to settle a controversy of this kind. What I wish to observe is this, that this same controversy (in common with the greater part of political questions) that agitates, excites, and unsettles the nations, would lose almost all its importance if the law had always been what it ought to be.

In fact, if law were confined to causing all persons, all liberties, and all properties to be respected—if it were merely the organization of individual right and individual defense—if it were the obstacle, the check, the chastisement opposed to all oppression, to all plunder—is it likely that we should dispute much, as citizens, on the subject of the greater or lesser universality of suffrage? Is it likely that it would compromise that greatest of advantages, the public peace? Is it likely that the excluded classes would not quietly wait for their turn? Is it likely that the enfranchised classes would be very jealous of their privilege? And is it not clear, that the interest of all being one and the same, some would act without much inconvenience to the others?

But if the fatal principle should come to be introduced, that, under pretense of organization, regulation, protection, or encouragement, the law may take from one party in order to give to another, help itself to the wealth acquired by all the classes that it may increase that of one class, whether that of the agriculturists, the manufacturers, the ship owners, or artists and comedians; then certainly, in this case, there is no class which may not try, and with reason, to place its hand upon the law, that would not demand with fury its right of election and eligibility, and that would overturn society rather than not obtain it. Even beggars and vagabonds will prove to you that they have an incontestable title to it. They will say:

> We never buy wine, tobacco, or salt, without paying the tax, and a part of this tax is given by law in perquisites and gratuities to men who are richer than we are. Others make use of the law to create an artificial rise in the price of bread, meat, iron, or cloth.
>
> Since everybody traffics in law for his own profit, we should like to do the same. We should like to make it produce the right to assistance, which is the poor man's plunder. To effect this, we ought to be electors and legislators, that we may organize, on a large scale, alms for our own class, as you have organized, on a large scale, protection for yours. Don't tell us that you will take our cause upon yourselves, and throw to us 600,000 francs to keep us quiet, like giving us a bone to pick. We have other claims, and, at any rate, we wish to stipulate for ourselves, as other classes have stipulated for themselves!

How is this argument to be answered? Yes, as long as it is admitted that the law may be diverted from its true mission, that it may violate property instead of securing it, everybody will be wanting to manufacture law, either to defend himself against plunder, or to organize it for his own profit. The political question will always be prejudicial, predominant, and absorbing; in a word, there will be fighting around the door of the Legislative Palace. The struggle will be no less furious within it. To be convinced of this, it is hardly necessary to look at what passes in the Chambers in France and in England; it is enough to know how the question stands.

Is there any need to prove that this odious perversion of law is a perpetual source of hatred and discord, that it even tends to social disorganization? Look at the United States. There is no country in the world where the law is kept more within its proper domain—which is, to secure to everyone his liberty and his property. Therefore, there is no country in the world where social order appears to rest upon a more solid basis. Nevertheless, even in the United States, there are two questions, and only two, that from the beginning have endangered political order. And what are these two questions? That of slavery and that of tariffs; that is, precisely the only two questions in which, contrary to the general spirit of this republic, law has taken the character of a plunderer. Slavery is a violation, sanctioned by law, of the rights of the person. Protection is a violation perpetrated by the law upon the rights of property; and certainly it is very remarkable that, in the midst of so many other debates, this double legal scourge, the sorrowful inheritance of the Old World, should be the only one which can, and perhaps will, cause the rupture of the Union. Indeed, a more astounding fact, in the heart of society, cannot be conceived than this: That law should have become an instrument of injustice. And if this fact occasions consequences so formidable to the United

States, where there is but one exception, what must it be with us in Europe, where it is a principle—a system?

Mr. Montalembert, adopting the thought of a famous proclamation of Mr. Carlier, said, "We must make war against socialism." And by socialism, according to the definition of Mr. Charles Dupin, he meant plunder. But what plunder did he mean? For there are two sorts: extralegal and legal plunder.

As to extralegal plunder, such as theft, or swindling, which is defined, foreseen, and punished by the penal code, I do not think it can be adorned by the name of socialism. It is not this that systematically threatens the foundations of society. Besides, the war against this kind of plunder has not waited for the signal of Mr. Montalembert or Mr. Carlier. It has gone on since the beginning of the world; France was carrying it on long before the revolution of February—long before the appearance of socialism—with all the ceremonies of magistracy, police, gendarmerie, prisons, dungeons, and scaffolds. It is the law itself that is conducting this war, and it is to be wished, in my opinion, that the law should always maintain this attitude with respect to plunder.

But this is not the case. The law sometimes takes its own part. Sometimes it accomplishes it with its own hands, in order to save the parties benefited the shame, the danger, and the scruple. Sometimes it places all this ceremony of magistracy, police, gendarmerie, and prisons, at the service of the plunderer, and treats the plundered party, when he defends himself, as the criminal. In a word, there is a legal plunder, and it is, no doubt, this that is meant by Mr. Montalembert.

This plunder may be only an exceptional blemish in the legislation of a people, and in this case, the best thing that can be done is, without so many speeches and lamentations, to do away with it as soon as possible, notwithstanding the clamors of interested parties. But how is it to be distinguished? Very easily. See whether the law takes from some persons that which belongs to them, to give to others what does not belong to them. See whether the law performs, for the profit of one citizen, and, to the injury of others, an act that this citizen cannot perform without committing a crime. Abolish this law without delay; it is not merely an iniquity—it is a fertile source of iniquities, for it invites reprisals; and if you do not take care, the exceptional case will extend, multiply, and become systematic. No doubt the party benefited will exclaim loudly; he will assert his acquired rights. He will say that the State is bound to protect and encourage his industry; he will plead that it is a good thing for the State to be enriched, that it may spend the more, and thus shower down salaries upon the poor workmen. Take care not to listen to this sophistry, for it is just by the systematizing of these arguments that legal plunder becomes systematized.

And this is what has taken place. The delusion of the day is to enrich all classes at the expense of each other; it is to generalize plunder under pretense of organizing it. Now, legal plunder may be exercised in an infinite multitude of ways. Hence come an infinite multitude of plans for organization; tariffs, protection, perquisites, gratuities, encouragements, progressive taxation, free public education, right to work, right to profit, right to wages, right to assistance, right to instruments of labor, gratuity of credit, etc., etc. And it is all these plans, taken as a whole, with what they have in common, legal plunder, that takes the name of socialism.

Now socialism, thus defined, and forming a doctrinal body, what other war would you make against it than a war of doctrine? You find this doctrine false, absurd, abominable. Refute it. This will be all the easier, the more false, absurd, and abominable it is. Above all, if you wish to be strong, begin by rooting out of your legislation every particle of socialism which may have crept into it—and this will be no light work.

Mr. Montalembert has been reproached with wishing to turn brute force against socialism. He ought to be exonerated from this reproach, for he has plainly said: "The war that we must make against socialism must be one that is compatible with the law, honor, and justice."

But how is it that Mr. Montalembert does not see that he is placing himself in a vicious circle? You would oppose law to socialism. But it is the law that socialism invokes. It aspires to legal, not extralegal plunder. It is of the law itself, like monopolists of all kinds, that it wants to make an instrument; and when once it has the law on its side, how will you be able to turn the law against it? How will you place it under the power of your tribunals, your gendarmes, and of your prisons? What will you do then? You wish to prevent it from taking any part in the making of laws. You would keep it outside the Legislative Palace. In this you will not succeed, I venture to prophesy, so long as legal plunder is the basis of the legislation within.

It is absolutely necessary that this question of legal plunder should be determined, and there are only three solutions of it:

1. When the few plunder the many.
2. When everybody plunders everybody else.
3. When nobody plunders anybody.

Partial plunder, universal plunder, absence of plunder, amongst these we have to make our choice. The law can only produce one of these results.

Partial plunder. This is the system that prevailed so long as the elective privilege was partial; a system that is resorted to, to avoid the invasion of socialism.

Universal plunder. We have been threatened by this system when the elective privilege has become universal; the masses having conceived the idea of making law, on the principle of legislators who had preceded them.

Absence of plunder. This is the principle of justice, peace, order, stability, conciliation, and of good sense, which I shall proclaim with all the force of my lungs (which is very inadequate, alas!) till the day of my death.

And, in all sincerity, can anything more be required at the hands of the law? Can the law, whose necessary sanction is force, be reasonably employed upon anything beyond securing to every one his right? I defy anyone to remove it from this circle without perverting it, and consequently turning force against right. And as this is the most fatal, the most illogical social perversion that can possibly be imagined, it must be admitted that the true solution, so much sought after, of the social problem, is contained in these simple words—LAW IS ORGANIZED JUSTICE.

Now it is important to remark, that to organize justice by law, that is to say by force, excludes the idea of organizing by law, or by force any manifestation whatever of human activity—labor, charity, agriculture, commerce, industry, instruction, the fine arts, or religion; for any one of these organizings would inevitably destroy the essential organization. How, in fact, can we imagine force encroaching upon the liberty of citizens without infringing upon justice, and so acting against its proper aim?

Here I am taking on the most popular prejudice of our time. It is not considered enough that law should be just, it must be philanthropic. It is not sufficient that it should guarantee to every citizen the free and inoffensive exercise of his faculties, applied to his physical, intellectual, and moral development; it is required to extend well-being, instruction, and morality, directly over the nation. This is the fascinating side of socialism.

But, I repeat it, these two missions of the law contradict each other. We have to choose between them. A citizen cannot at the same time be free and not free. Mr. de Lamartine wrote to me one day thus: "Your doctrine is only the half of my program; you have stopped at liberty, I go on to fraternity." I answered him: "The second part of your program will destroy the first." And in fact it is impossible for me to separate the word fraternity from the word voluntary. I cannot possibly conceive fraternity legally enforced, without liberty being legally destroyed, and justice legally trampled under foot. Legal plunder has two roots: one of them, as we have already seen, is in human greed; the other is in misconceived philanthropy.

Before I proceed, I think I ought to explain myself upon the word plunder.

I do not take it, as it often is taken, in a vague, undefined, relative, or metaphorical sense. I use it in its scientific acceptation, and as expressing the opposite idea to property. When a portion of wealth passes out of the hands of him who has acquired it, without his consent, and without compensation, to him who has not created it, whether by force or by artifice, I say that property is violated, that plunder is perpetrated. I say that this is exactly what the law ought to repress always and everywhere. If the law itself performs the action it ought to repress, I say that plunder is still perpetrated, and even, in a social point of view, under aggravated circumstances. In this case, however, he who profits from the plunder is not responsible for it; it is the law, the lawgiver, society itself, and this is where the political danger lies.

It is to be regretted that there is something offensive in the word. I have sought in vain for another, for I would not wish at any time, and especially just now, to add an irritating word to our disagreements; therefore, whether I am believed or not, I declare that I do not mean to impugn the intentions nor the morality of anybody. I am attacking an idea that I believe to be false—a system that appears to me to be unjust; and this is so independent of intentions, that each of us profits by it without wishing it, and suffers from it without being aware of the cause.

Any person must write under the influence of party spirit or of fear, who would call into question the sincerity of protectionism, of socialism, and even of communism, which are one and the same plant, in three different periods of its growth. All that can be said is, that plunder is more visible by its partiality in protectionism,[3] and by its universality in communism; whence it follows that, of the three systems, socialism is still the most vague, the most undefined, and consequently the most sincere.

Be that as it may, to conclude that legal plunder has one of its roots in misconceived philanthropy, is evidently to put intentions out of the question.

---

[3]If protection were only granted in France to a single class, to the engineers, for instance, it would be so absurdly plundering, as to be unable to maintain itself. Thus we see all the protected trades combine, make common cause, and even recruit themselves in such a way as to appear to embrace the mass of the national labor. They feel instinctively that plunder is slurred over by being generalized.

With this understanding, let us examine the value, the origin, and the tendency of this popular aspiration, which pretends to realize the general good by general plunder.

The Socialists say, since the law organizes justice, why should it not organize labor, instruction, and religion?

Why? Because it could not organize labor, instruction, and religion, without disorganizing justice.

For remember, that law is force, and that consequently the domain of the law cannot properly extend beyond the domain of force.

When law and force keep a man within the bounds of justice, they impose nothing upon him but a mere negation. They only oblige him to abstain from doing harm. They violate neither his personality, his liberty, nor his property. They only guard the personality, the liberty, the property of others. They hold themselves on the defensive; they defend the equal right of all. They fulfill a mission whose harmlessness is evident, whose utility is palpable, and whose legitimacy is not to be disputed. This is so true that, as a friend of mine once remarked to me, to say that the aim of the law is to cause justice to reign, is to use an expression that is not rigorously exact. It ought to be said, the aim of the law is to prevent injustice from reigning. In fact, it is not justice that has an existence of its own, it is injustice. The one results from the absence of the other.

But when the law, through the medium of its necessary agent—force—imposes a form of labor, a method or a subject of instruction, a creed, or a worship, it is no longer negative; it acts positively upon men. It substitutes the will of the legislator for their own will, the initiative of the legislator for their own initiative. They have no need to consult, to compare, or to foresee; the law does all that for them. The intellect is for them a useless encumbrance; they cease to be men; they lose their personality, their liberty, their property.

Try to imagine a form of labor imposed by force, that is not a violation of liberty; a transmission of wealth imposed by force, that is not a violation of property. If you cannot succeed in reconciling this, you are bound to conclude that the law cannot organize labor and industry without organizing injustice.

When, from the seclusion of his office, a politician takes a view of society, he is struck with the spectacle of inequality that presents itself. He mourns over the sufferings that are the lot of so many of our brethren, sufferings whose aspect is rendered yet more sorrowful by the contrast of luxury and wealth.

He ought, perhaps, to ask himself whether such a social state has not been caused by the plunder of ancient times, exercised in the way of conquests; and by plunder of more recent times, effected through the medium of the laws? He ought to ask himself whether, granting the aspiration of all men to well-being and improvement, the reign of justice would not suffice to realize the greatest activity of progress, and the greatest amount of equality compatible with that individual responsibility that God has awarded as a just retribution of virtue and vice?

He never gives this a thought. His mind turns towards combinations, arrangements, legal or factitious organizations. He seeks the remedy in perpetuating and exaggerating what has produced the evil.

For, justice apart, which we have seen is only a negation, is there any one of these legal arrangements that does not contain the principle of plunder?

You say, "There are men who have no money," and you apply to the law. But the law is not a self-supplied fountain, whence every stream may obtain supplies independently of society. Nothing can enter the public treasury, in favor of one citizen or one class, but what other citizens and other classes have been forced to send to it. If everyone draws from it only the equivalent of what he has contributed to it, your law, it is true, is no plunderer, but it does nothing for men who want money—it does not promote equality. It can only be an instrument of equalization as far as it takes from one party to give to another, and then it is an instrument of plunder. Examine, in this light, the protection of tariffs, subsidies, right to profit, right to labor, right to assistance, free public education, progressive taxation, gratuitousness of credit, social workshops, and you will always find at the bottom legal plunder, organized injustice.

You say, "There are men who want knowledge," and you apply to the law. But the law is not a torch that sheds light that originates within itself. It extends over a society where there are men who have knowledge, and others who have not; citizens who want to learn, and others who are disposed to teach. It can only do one of two things: either allow a free operation to this kind of transaction, i.e., let this kind of want satisfy itself freely; or else preempt the will of the people in the matter, and take from some of them sufficient to pay professors commissioned to instruct others for free. But, in this second case there cannot fail to be a violation of liberty and property—legal plunder.

You say, "Here are men who are wanting in morality or religion," and you apply to the law; but law is force, and need I say how far it is a violent and absurd enterprise to introduce force in these matters?

As the result of its systems and of its efforts, it would seem that socialism, notwithstanding all its self-complacency, can scarcely help perceiving the monster of legal plunder. But what does it do? It disguises it cleverly from others, and even from itself, under the seductive names of fraternity, solidarity, organization, association. And because we do not ask so much at the hands of the law, because we only ask it for justice, it alleges that we reject fraternity, solidarity, organization, and association; and they brand us with the name of individualists.

We can assure them that what we repudiate is not natural organization, but forced organization.

It is not free association, but the forms of association that they would impose upon us.

It is not spontaneous fraternity, but legal fraternity.

It is not providential solidarity, but artificial solidarity, which is only an unjust displacement of responsibility.

Socialism, like the old policy from which it emanates, confounds Government and society. And so, every time we object to a thing being done by Government, it concludes that we object to its being done at all. We disapprove of education by the State—then we are against education altogether. We object to a State religion—then we would have no religion at all. We object to an equality which is brought about by the State then we are against equality, etc., etc. They might as well accuse us of wishing men not to eat, because we object to the cultivation of corn by the State.

How is it that the strange idea of making the law produce what it does not contain—prosperity, in a positive sense, wealth, science, religion—should ever have gained ground in the political world? The modern politicians, particularly those of the Socialist school, found their different theories upon one common hypothesis; and surely a more strange, a more presumptuous notion, could never have entered a human brain.

They divide mankind into two parts. Men in general, except one, form the first; the politician himself forms the second, which is by far the most important.

In fact, they begin by supposing that men are devoid of any principle of action, and of any means of discernment in themselves; that they have no initiative; that they are inert matter, passive particles, atoms without impulse; at best a vegetation indifferent to its own mode of existence, susceptible of assuming, from an exterior will and hand an infinite number of forms, more or less symmetrical, artistic, and perfected.

Moreover, every one of these politicians does not hesitate to assume that he himself is, under the names of organizer, discoverer, legislator, institutor or founder, this will and hand, this universal initiative, this creative power, whose sublime mission it is to gather together these scattered materials, that is, men, into society.

Starting from these data, as a gardener according to his caprice shapes his trees into pyramids, parasols, cubes, cones, vases, espaliers, distaffs, or fans; so the Socialist, following his chimera, shapes poor humanity into groups, series, circles, subcircles, honeycombs, or social workshops, with all kinds of variations. And as the gardener, to bring his trees into shape, needs hatchets, pruning hooks, saws, and shears, so the politician, to bring society into shape, needs the forces which he can only find in the laws; the law of tariffs, the law of taxation, the law of assistance, and the law of education.

It is so true, that the Socialists look upon mankind as a subject for social experiments, that if, by chance, they are not quite certain of the success of these experiments, they will request a portion of mankind, as a subject to experiment upon. It is well known how popular the idea of trying all systems is, and one of their chiefs has been known seriously to demand of the Constituent Assembly a parish, with all its inhabitants, upon which to make his experiments.

It is thus that an inventor will make a small machine before he makes one of the regular size. Thus the chemist sacrifices some substances, the agriculturist some seed and a corner of his field, to make trial of an idea.

But think of the difference between the gardener and his trees, between the inventor and his machine, between the chemist and his substances, between the agriculturist and his seed! The Socialist thinks, in all sincerity, that there is the same difference between himself and mankind.

No wonder the politicians of the nineteenth century look upon society as an artificial production of the legislator's genius. This idea, the result of a classical education, has taken possession of all the thinkers and great writers of our country.

To all these persons, the relations between mankind and the legislator appear to be the same as those that exist between the clay and the potter.

Moreover, if they have consented to recognize in the heart of man a capability of action, and in his intellect a faculty of discernment, they have looked upon this gift of God as a fatal one, and thought that mankind, under these two impulses, tended fatally towards ruin. They have taken it for granted that if abandoned to their own inclinations, men would only occupy themselves with religion to arrive at atheism, with instruction to come to ignorance, and with labor and exchange to be extinguished in misery.

Happily, according to these writers, there are some men, termed governors and legislators, upon whom Heaven has bestowed opposite tendencies, not for their own sake only, but for the sake of the rest of the world.

Whilst mankind tends to evil, they incline to good; whilst mankind is advancing towards darkness, they are aspiring to enlightenment; whilst mankind is drawn towards vice, they are attracted by virtue. And, this granted, they demand the assistance of force, by means of which they are to substitute their own tendencies for those of the human race.

It is only needful to open, almost at random, a book on philosophy, politics, or history, to see how strongly this idea—the child of classical studies and the mother of socialism—is rooted in our country; that mankind is merely inert matter, receiving life, organization, morality, and wealth from power; or, rather, and still worse—that mankind itself tends towards degradation, and is only arrested in its tendency by the mysterious hand of the legislator. Classical conventionalism shows us everywhere, behind passive society, a hidden power, under the names of Law, or Legislator (or, by a mode of expression which refers to some person or persons of undisputed weight and authority, but not named), which moves, animates, enriches, and regenerates mankind.

We will give a quotation from Bossuet:

> One of the things which was the most strongly impressed (by whom?) upon the mind of the Egyptians, was the love of their country. . . . Nobody was allowed to be useless to the State; the law assigned to every one his employment, which descended from father to son. No one was permitted to have two professions, nor to adopt another. . . . But there was one occupation which was

> obliged to be common to all, this was the study of the laws and of wisdom; ignorance of religion and the political regulations of the country was excused in no condition of life. Moreover, every profession had a district assigned to it (by whom?). . . . Amongst good laws, one of the best things was, that everybody was taught to observe them (by whom?). Egypt abounded with wonderful inventions, and nothing was neglected which could render life comfortable and tranquil.

Thus men, according to Bossuet, derive nothing from themselves; patriotism, wealth, inventions, husbandry, science—all come to them by the operation of the laws, or by kings. All they have to do is to be passive. It is on this ground that Bossuet takes exception when Diodorus accuses the Egyptians of rejecting wrestling and music. "How is that possible," says he, "since these arts were invented by Trismegistus?"

It is the same with the Persians:

> One of the first cares of the prince was to encourage agriculture. . . . As there were posts established for the regulation of the armies, so there were offices for the superintending of rural works. . . . The respect with which the Persians were inspired for royal authority was excessive.

The Greeks, although full of mind, were no less strangers to their own responsibilities; so much so, that of themselves, like dogs and horses, they would not have ventured upon the most simple games. In a classical sense, it is an undisputed thing that everything comes to the people from without.

> The Greeks, naturally full of spirit and courage, had been early cultivated by kings and colonies who had come from Egypt. From them they had

> learned the exercises of the body, foot races, and horse and chariot races. . . . The best thing that the Egyptians had taught them was to become docile, and to allow themselves to be formed by the laws for the public good.

FÉNELON—Reared in the study and admiration of antiquity and a witness of the power of Louis XIV, Fenelon naturally adopted the idea that mankind should be passive, and that its misfortunes and its prosperities, its virtues and its vices, are caused by the external influence that is exercised upon it by the law, or by the makers of the law. Thus, in his Utopia of Salentum, he brings the men, with their interests, their faculties, their desires, and their possessions, under the absolute direction of the legislator. Whatever the subject may be, they themselves have no voice in it—the prince judges for them. The nation is just a shapeless mass, of which the prince is the soul. In him resides the thought, the foresight, the principle of all organization, of all progress; on him, therefore, rests all the responsibility.

In proof of this assertion, I might transcribe the whole of the tenth book of *Telemachus*. I refer the reader to it, and shall content myself with quoting some passages taken at random from this celebrated work, to which, in every other respect, I am the first to render justice.

With the astonishing credulity that characterizes the classics, Fénelon, against the authority of reason and of facts, admits the general felicity of the Egyptians, and attributes it, not to their own wisdom, but to that of their kings:

> We could not turn our eyes to the two shores, without perceiving rich towns and country seats, agreeably situated; fields that were covered every year,

> without intermission, with golden crops; meadows full of flocks; laborers bending under the weight of fruits that the earth lavished on its cultivators; and shepherds who made the echoes around repeat the soft sounds of their pipes and flutes. "Happy," said Mentor, "is that people who is governed by a wise king.". . . Mentor afterwards desired me to remark the happiness and abundance that was spread over all the country of Egypt, where twenty-two thousand cities might be counted. He admired the excellent police regulations of the cities; the justice administered in favor of the poor against the rich; the good education of the children, who were accustomed to obedience, labor, and the love of arts and letters; the exactness with which all the ceremonies of religion were performed; the disinterestedness, the desire of honor, the fidelity to men, and the fear of the gods, with which every father inspired his children. He could not sufficiently admire the prosperous state of the country. "Happy" said he, "is the people whom a wise king rules in such a manner."

Fénelon's idyll on Crete is still more fascinating. Mentor is made to say:

> All that you will see in this wonderful island is the result of the laws of Minos. The education that the children receive renders the body healthy and robust. They are accustomed, from the first, to a frugal and laborious life; it is supposed that all the pleasures of sense enervate the body and the mind; no other pleasure is presented to them but that of being invincible by virtue, that of acquiring much glory . . . there they punish three vices that go unpunished amongst other people—ingratitude, dissimulation, and avarice. As to pomp and dissipation, there is no need to punish these, for they are unknown in Crete. . . . No costly furniture, no magnificent clothing, no delicious feasts, no gilded palaces are allowed.

It is thus that Mentor prepares his scholar to mould and manipulate, doubtless with the most philanthropic intentions, the people of Ithaca, and, to confirm him in these ideas, he gives him the example of Salentum.

So we receive our first political notions. We are taught to treat men very much as Oliver de Serres teaches farmers to manage and to mix the soil.

MONTESQUIEU—

> To sustain the spirit of commerce, it is necessary that all the laws should favor it; that these same laws, by their regulations in dividing the fortunes in proportion as commerce enlarges them, should place every poor citizen in sufficiently easy circumstances to enable him to work like the others, and every rich citizen in such mediocrity that he must work, in order to retain or to acquire.

Thus the laws are to dispose of all fortunes.

> Although in a democracy, real equality be the soul of the State, yet it is so difficult to establish that an extreme exactness in this matter would not always be desirable. It is sufficient that a census be established to reduce or fix the differences to a certain point, after which, it is for particular laws to equalize, as it were, the inequality by burdens imposed upon the rich and reliefs granted to the poor.

Here, again, we see the equalization of fortunes by law, that is, by force.

> There were, in Greece, two kinds of republics. One was military, as Sparta; the other commercial, as Athens. In the one it was wished (by whom?) that the citizens should be idle: in the other, the love of labor was encouraged.
>
> It is worth our while to pay a little attention to the extent of genius required by these legislators, that

we may see how, by confounding all the virtues, they showed their wisdom to the world. Lycurgus, blending theft with the spirit of justice, the hardest slavery with extreme liberty, the most atrocious sentiments with the greatest moderation, gave stability to his city. He seemed to deprive it of all its resources, arts, commerce, money, and walls; there was ambition without the hope of rising; there were natural sentiments where the individual was neither child, nor husband, nor father. Chastity even was deprived of modesty. By this road Sparta was led on to grandeur and to glory.

The phenomenon that we observe in the institutions of Greece has been seen in the midst of the degeneracy and corruption of our modern times. An honest legislator has formed a people where probity has appeared as natural as bravery among the Spartans. Mr. Penn is a true Lycurgus, and although the former had peace for his object, and the latter war, they resemble each other in the singular path along which they have led their people, in their influence over free men, in the prejudices which they have overcome, the passions they have subdued.

Paraguay furnishes us with another example. Society has been accused of the crime of regarding the pleasure of commanding as the only good of life; but it will always be a noble thing to govern men by making them happy.

Those who desire to form similar institutions will establish community of property, as in the republic of Plato, the same reverence as he enjoined for the gods, separation from strangers for the preservation of morality, and make the city and not the citizens create commerce: they should give our arts without our luxury, our wants without our desires.

Vulgar infatuation may exclaim, if it likes, "It is Montesquieu! magnificent! sublime!" I am not afraid to express my opinion, and to say:

> What! You have the gall to call that fine? It is frightful! It is abominable! And these extracts, which I might multiply, show that according to Montesquieu, the persons, the liberties, the property, mankind itself, are nothing but grist for the mill of the sagacity of lawgivers.

ROUSSEAU—Although this politician, the paramount authority of the Democrats, makes the social edifice rest upon the general will, no one has so completely admitted the hypothesis of the entire passiveness of human nature in the presence of the lawgiver:

> If it is true that a great prince is a rare thing, how much more so must a great lawgiver be? The former has only to follow the pattern proposed to him by the latter. This latter is the engineer who invents the machine; the former is merely the workman who sets it in motion.

And what part have men to act in all this? That of the machine, which is set in motion; or rather, are they not the brute matter of which the machine is made? Thus, between the legislator and the prince, between the prince and his subjects, there are the same relations as those that exist between the agricultural writer and the agriculturist, the agriculturist and the clod. At what a vast height, then, is the politician placed, who rules over legislators themselves and teaches them their trade in such imperative terms as the following:

> Would you give consistency to the State? Bring the extremes together as much as possible. Suffer neither wealthy persons nor beggars.

> If the soil is poor and barren, or the country too much confined for the inhabitants, turn to industry and the arts, whose productions you will exchange for the provisions which you require. . . . On a good soil, if you are short of inhabitants, give all your attention to agriculture, which multiplies men, and banish the arts, which only serve to depopulate the country. . . . Pay attention to extensive and convenient coasts. Cover the sea with vessels, and you will have a brilliant and short existence. If your seas wash only inaccessible rocks, let the people be barbarous, and eat fish; they will live more quietly, perhaps better, and most certainly more happily. In short, besides those maxims which are common to all, every people has its own particular circumstances, which demand a legislation peculiar to itself.
>
> It was thus that the Hebrews formerly, and the Arabs more recently, had religion for their principal object; that of the Athenians was literature; that of Carthage and Tyre, commerce; of Rhodes, naval affairs; of Sparta, war; and of Rome, virtue. The author of the "Spirit of Laws" has shown the art by which the legislator should frame his institutions towards each of these objects. . . . But if the legislator, mistaking his object, should take up a principle different from that which arises from the nature of things; if one should tend to slavery, and the other to liberty; if one to wealth, and the other to population; one to peace, and the other to conquests; the laws will insensibly become enfeebled, the Constitution will be impaired, and the State will be subject to incessant agitations until it is destroyed, or becomes changed, and invincible Nature regains her empire.

But if Nature is sufficiently invincible to regain its empire, why does not Rousseau admit that it had no need of the legislator to gain its empire from the beginning?

Why does he not allow that by obeying their own impulse, men would of themselves apply agriculture to a fertile district, and commerce to extensive and commodious coasts without the interference of a Lycurgus, a Solon, or a Rousseau, who would undertake it at the risk of deceiving themselves?

Be that as it may, we see with what a terrible responsibility Rousseau invests inventors, institutors, conductors, and manipulators of societies. He is, therefore, very exacting with regard to them.

> He who dares to undertake the institutions of a people, ought to feel that he can, as it were, transform every individual, who is by himself a perfect and solitary whole, receiving his life and being from a larger whole of which he forms a part; he must feel that he can change the constitution of man, to fortify it, and substitute a social and moral existence for the physical and independent one that we have all received from nature. In a word, he must deprive man of his own powers, to give him others that are foreign to him.

Poor human nature! What would become of its dignity if it were entrusted to the disciples of Rousseau?

RAYNAL—

> The climate, that is, the air and the soil, is the first element for the legislator. His resources prescribe to him his duties. First, he must consult his local position. A population dwelling upon maritime shores must have laws fitted for navigation. . . . If the colony is located in an inland region, a legislator must provide for the nature of the soil, and for its degree of fertility. . . .
>
> It is more especially in the distribution of property that the wisdom of legislation will appear. As a

> general rule, and in every country, when a new colony is founded, land should be given to each man, sufficient for the support of his family. . . .
>
> In an uncultivated island, which you are colonizing with children, it will only be needful to let the germs of truth expand in the developments of reason! . . . But when you establish old people in a new country, the skill consists in only allowing it those injurious opinions and customs which it is impossible to cure and correct. If you wish to prevent them from being perpetuated, you will act upon the rising generation by a general and public education of the children. A prince or legislator ought never to found a colony without previously sending wise men there to instruct the youth.... In a new colony, every facility is open to the precautions of the legislator who desires to purify the tone and the manners of the people. If he has genius and virtue, the lands and the men that are at his disposal will inspire his soul with a plan of society that a writer can only vaguely trace, and in a way that would be subject to the instability of all hypotheses, which are varied and complicated by an infinity of circumstances too difficult to foresee and to combine.

One would think it was a professor of agriculture who was saying to his pupils

> The climate is the only rule for the agriculturist. His resources dictate to him his duties. The first thing he has to consider is his local position. If he is on a clayey soil, he must do so and so. If he has to contend with sand, this is the way in which he must set about it. Every facility is open to the agriculturist who wishes to clear and improve his soil. If he only has the skill, the manure which he has at his disposal will suggest to him a plan of operation, which a professor can only vaguely trace, and in a way that would be subject to the uncertainty of all hypotheses, which vary and are complicated by an

> infinity of circumstances too difficult to foresee and to combine.

But, oh! sublime writers, deign to remember sometimes that this clay, this sand, this manure, of which you are disposing in so arbitrary a manner, are men, your equals, intelligent and free beings like yourselves, who have received from God, as you have, the faculty of seeing, of foreseeing, of thinking, and of judging for themselves!

MABLY—(He is supposing the laws to be worn out by time and by the neglect of security, and continues thus):

> Under these circumstances, we must be convinced that the bonds of Government are slack. Give them a new tension (it is the reader who is addressed), and the evil will be remedied. . . . Think less of punishing the faults than of encouraging the virtues that you want. By this method you will bestow upon your republic the vigor of youth. Through ignorance of this, a free people has lost its liberty! But if the evil has made so much way that the ordinary magistrates are unable to remedy it effectually, have recourse to an extraordinary magistracy, whose time should be short, and its power considerable. The imagination of the citizens requires to be impressed.

In this style he goes on through twenty volumes.

There was a time when, under the influence of teaching like this, which is the foundation of classical education, everyone was for placing himself beyond and above mankind, for the sake of arranging, organizing, and instituting it in his own way.

CONDILLAC—

> Take upon yourself, my lord, the character of Lycurgus or of Solon. Before you finish reading

> this essay, amuse yourself with giving laws to some wild people in America or in Africa. Establish these roving men in fixed dwellings; teach them to keep flocks. . . . Endeavor to develop the social qualities that nature has implanted in them. . . . Make them begin to practice the duties of humanity. . . . Cause the pleasures of the passions to become distasteful to them by punishments, and you will see these barbarians, with every plan of your legislation, lose a vice and gain a virtue.
>
> All these people have had laws. But few among them have been happy. Why is this? Because legislators have almost always been ignorant of the object of society, which is to unite families by a common interest.
>
> Impartiality in law consists in two things, in establishing equality in the fortunes and in the dignity of the citizens. . . . In proportion to the degree of equality established by the laws, the dearer will they become to every citizen. How can avarice, ambition, dissipation, idleness, sloth, envy, hatred, or jealousy agitate men who are equal in fortune and dignity, and to whom the laws leave no hope of disturbing their equality?
>
> What has been told you of the republic of Sparta ought to enlighten you on this question. No other State has had laws more in accordance with the order of nature or of equality.

It is not to be wondered at that the seventeeth and eighteenth centuries should have looked upon the human race as inert matter, ready to receive everything—form, figure, impulse, movement, and life, from a great prince, or a great legislator, or a great genius. These ages were reared in the study of antiquity; and antiquity presents everywhere—in Egypt, Persia, Greece, and Rome, the spectacle of a few men molding mankind according to their fancy, and mankind to this end enslaved by force or by imposture. And what does this prove? That because men and society are improvable, error, ignorance, despotism, slavery, and superstition must be more prevalent in early times. The mistake of the writers quoted above is not that they have asserted this fact, but that they have proposed it as a rule for the admiration and imitation of future generations. Their mistake has been, with an inconceivable absence of discernment, and upon the faith of a puerile conventionalism, that they have admitted what is inadmissible, viz., the grandeur, dignity, morality, and well-being of the artificial societies of the ancient world; they have not understood that time produces and spreads enlightenment; and that in proportion to the increase of enlightenment, right ceases to be upheld by force, and society regains possession of herself.

And, in fact, what is the political work that we are endeavoring to promote? It is no other than the instinctive effort of every people towards liberty. And what is liberty, whose name can make every heart beat, and which can agitate the world, but the union of all liberties, the liberty of conscience, of education, of association, of the press, of movement, of labor, and of exchange; in other words, the free exercise, for all, of all the inoffensive faculties; and again, in other words, the destruction of all despotisms, even of legal despotism, and the reduction of law to its only rational sphere, which is to regulate the individual right of legitimate defense, or to repress injustice?

This tendency of the human race, it must be admitted, is greatly thwarted, particularly in our country, by the fatal disposition, resulting from classical teaching and common to all politicians, of placing themselves beyond mankind, to arrange, organize, and regulate it, according to their fancy.

For whilst society is struggling to realize liberty, the great men who place themselves at its head, imbued with the principles of the seventeenth and eighteenth centuries, think only of subjecting it to the philanthropic despotism of their social inventions, and making it bear with docility, according to the expression of Rousseau, the yoke of public felicity as pictured in their own imaginations.

This was particularly the case in 1789. No sooner was the old system destroyed than society was to be submitted to other artificial arrangements, always with the same starting point—the omnipotence of the law.

SAINT-JUST—

> The legislator commands the future. It is for him to will for the good of mankind. It is for him to make men what he wishes them to be.

ROBESPIERRE—

> The function of Government is to direct the physical and moral powers of the nation towards the object of its institution.

BILLAUD VARENNES—

> A people who are to be restored to liberty must be formed anew. Ancient prejudices must be destroyed, antiquated customs changed, depraved affections corrected, inveterate vices eradicated. For this, a strong force and a vehement impulse will be necessary. . . . Citizens, the inflexible austerity of Lycurgus created the firm basis of the Spartan republic. The feeble and trusting disposition of Solon plunged Athens into slavery. This parallel contains the whole science of Government.

LEPELLETIER—

> Considering the extent of human degradation, I am convinced—of the necessity of effecting an entire regeneration of the race, and, if I may so express myself, of creating a new people.

Men, therefore, are nothing but raw material. It is not for them to will their own improvement. They are not capable of it; according to Saint-Just, it is only the legislator who is. Men are merely to be what he wills that they should be. According to Robespierre, who copies Rousseau literally, the legislator is to begin by assigning the aim of the institutions of the nation. After this, the Government has only to direct all its physical and moral forces towards this end. All this time the nation itself is to remain perfectly passive; and Billaud Varennes would teach us that it ought to have no prejudices, affections, nor wants, but such as are authorized by the legislator. He even goes so far as to say that the inflexible austerity of a man is the basis of a republic.

We have seen that, in cases where the evil is so great that the ordinary magistrates are unable to remedy it, Mably recommends a dictatorship, to promote virtue. "Have recourse," says he, "to an extraordinary magistracy, whose time shall be short, and his power considerable. The imagination of the people requires to be impressed." This doctrine has not been neglected. Listen to Robespierre:

> The principle of the Republican Government is virtue, and the means to be adopted, during its establishment, is terror. We want to substitute, in our country, morality for self-indulgence, probity for honor, principles for customs, duties for decorum, the empire of reason for the tyranny of

> fashion, contempt of vice for contempt of misfortune, pride for insolence, greatness of soul for vanity, love of glory for love of money, good people for good company, merit for intrigue, genius for wit, truth for glitter, the charm of happiness for the weariness of pleasure, the greatness of man for the littleness of the great, a magnanimous, powerful, happy people, for one that is easy, frivolous, degraded; that is to say, we would substitute all the virtues and miracles of a republic for all the vices and absurdities of monarchy.

At what a vast height above the rest of mankind does Robespierre place himself here! And observe the arrogance with which he speaks. He is not content with expressing a desire for a great renovation of the human heart, he does not even expect such a result from a regular Government. No; he intends to effect it himself, and by means of terror. The object of the discourse from which this puerile and laborious mass of antithesis is extracted, was to exhibit the principles of morality that ought to direct a revolutionary Government. Moreover, when Robespierre asks for a dictatorship, it is not merely for the purpose of repelling a foreign enemy, or of putting down factions; it is that he may establish, by means of terror and as a preliminary to the operation of the Constitution, his own principles of morality. He pretends to nothing short of extirpating from the country by means of terror, self-interest, honor, customs, decorum, fashion, vanity, the love of money, good company, intrigue, wit, luxury, and misery. It is not until after he, Robespierre, shall have accomplished these miracles, as he rightly calls them, that he will allow the law to regain her empire. Truly it would be well if these visionaries, who think so much of themselves and so little of mankind, who want to renew everything, would only be content with trying to reform themselves, the task would be arduous enough for them. In general, however, these gentlemen, the reformers, legislators, and politicians, do not desire to exercise an immediate despotism over mankind. No, they are too moderate and too philanthropic for that. They only contend for the despotism, the absolutism, the omnipotence of the law. They aspire only to make the law.

To show how universal this strange disposition has been in France, I had need not only to have copied the whole of the works of Mably, Raynal, Rousseau, Fenelon, and to have made long extracts from Bossuet and Montesquieu, but to have given the entire transactions of the sittings of the Convention. I shall do no such thing, however, but merely refer the reader to them.

No wonder this idea suited Bonaparte so well. He embraced it with ardor, and put it in practice with energy. Playing the part of a chemist, Europe was to him the material for his experiments. But this material reacted against him. More than half undeceived, Bonaparte, at St. Helena, seemed to admit that there is an initiative in every people, and he became less hostile to liberty. Yet this did not prevent him from giving this lesson to his son in his will—"To govern is to diffuse morality, education, and well-being."

After all this, I hardly need show, by fastidious quotations, the opinions of Morelly, Babeuf, Owen, Saint Simon, and Fourier. I shall confine myself to a few extracts from Louis Blanc's book on the organization of labor.

"In our project, society receives the impulse of power."

In what does the impulse that power gives to society consist? In imposing upon it the project of Mr. Louis Blanc.

On the other hand, society is the human race. The human race, then, is to receive its impulse from Mr. Louis Blanc.

It is at liberty to do so or not, it will be said. Of course the human race is at liberty to take advice from anybody, whoever it may be. But this is not the way in which Mr. Louis Blanc understands the thing. He means that his project should be converted into law, and consequently forcibly imposed by power.

> In our project, the State has only to give a legislation to labor, by means of which the industrial movement may and ought to be accomplished in all liberty. It (the State) merely places society on an incline (that is all) that it may descend, when once it is placed there, by the mere force of things, and by the natural course of the established mechanism.

But what is this incline? One indicated by Mr. Louis Blanc. Does it not lead to an abyss? No, it leads to happiness. Why, then, does not society go there of itself? Because it does not know what it wants, and it requires an impulse. What is to give it this impulse? Power. And who is to give the impulse to power? The inventor of the machine, Mr. Louis Blanc.

We shall never get out of this circle—mankind passive, and a great man moving it by the intervention of the law. Once on this incline, will society enjoy something like liberty? Without a doubt. And what is liberty?

> Once for all: liberty consists not only in the right granted, but in the power given to man to exercise, to develop his faculties under the empire of justice, and under the protection of the law.
>
> And this is no vain distinction; there is a deep meaning in it, and its consequences are imponderable. For

> when once it is admitted that man, to be truly free, must have the power to exercise and develop his faculties, it follows that every member of society has a claim upon it for such education as shall enable his faculties to display themselves, and for the tools of labor, without which human activity can find no scope. Now, by whose intervention is society to give to each of its members the requisite education and the necessary tools of labor, unless by that of the State?

Thus, liberty is power. In what does this power consist? In possessing education and tools of labor. Who is to give education and tools of labor? Society, who owes them. By whose intervention is society to give tools of labor to those who do not possess them? By the intervention of the State. From whom is the State to obtain them?

It is for the reader to answer this question, and to notice whither all this tends.

One of the strangest phenomena of our time, and one that will probably be a matter of astonishment to our descendants, is the doctrine which is founded upon this triple hypothesis: the radical passiveness of mankind,—the omnipotence of the law,—the infallibility of the legislator: this is the sacred symbol of the party that proclaims itself exclusively democratic.

It is true that it professes also to be social.

So far as it is democratic, it has an unlimited faith in mankind.

So far as it is social, it places mankind beneath the mud.

Are political rights under discussion? Is a legislator to be chosen? Oh, then the people possess science by instinct: they are gifted with an admirable discernment; their will is always right; the general will cannot err. Suffrage cannot be too universal. Nobody is under any responsibility to society. The will and the capacity to choose well are taken for granted. Can the people be mistaken? Are we not living in an age of enlightenment? What! Are the people to be forever led about by the nose? Have they not acquired their rights at the cost of effort and sacrifice? Have they not given sufficient proof of intelligence and wisdom? Are they not arrived at maturity? Are they not in a state to judge for themselves? Do they not know their own interest? Is there a man or a class who would dare to claim the right of putting himself in the place of the people, of deciding and of acting for them? No, no; the people would be free, and they shall be so. They wish to conduct their own affairs, and they shall do so.

But when once the legislator is duly elected, then indeed the style of his speech alters. The nation is sent back into passiveness, inertness, nothingness, and the legislator takes possession of omnipotence. It is for him to invent, for him to direct, for him to impel, for him to organize. Mankind has nothing to do but to submit; the hour of despotism has struck. And we must observe that this is decisive; for the people, just before so enlightened, so moral, so perfect, have no inclinations at all, or, if they have any, these all lead them downwards towards degradation. And yet they ought to have a little liberty! But are we not assured by Mr. Considerant that liberty leads fatally to monopoly? Are we not told that liberty is competition? and that competition, according to Mr. Louis Blanc, is a system of extermination for the people, and of ruination for trade? For that reason people are exterminated and ruined in proportion as they are free—take, for example, Switzerland, Holland, England, and the United States? Does not Mr. Louis Blanc tell us again that competition leads to monopoly, and that, for the same reason, cheapness leads to exorbitant prices? That competition tends to drain the sources of consumption, and diverts production to a destructive activity? That competition forces production to increase, and consumption to decrease—whence it follows that free people produce for the sake of not consuming; that there is nothing but oppression and madness among them; and that it is absolutely necessary for Mr. Louis Blanc to see to it?

What sort of liberty should be allowed to men? Liberty of conscience?—But we should see them all profiting by the permission to become atheists. Liberty of education?—But parents would be paying professors to teach their sons immorality and error; besides, if we are to believe Mr. Thiers, education, if left to the national liberty, would cease to be national, and we should be educating our children in the ideas of the Turks or Hindus, instead of which, thanks to the legal despotism of the universities, they have the good fortune to be educated in the noble ideas of the Romans. Liberty of labor? But this is only competition, whose effect is to leave all products unconsumed, to exterminate the people, and to ruin the tradesmen. The liberty of exchange? But it is well known that the protectionists have shown, over and over again, that a man will inevitably be ruined when he exchanges freely, and that to become rich it is necessary to exchange without liberty. Liberty of association? But according to the socialist doctrine, liberty and association exclude each other, for the liberty of men is attacked just to force them to associate.

You must see, then, that the socialist democrats cannot in conscience allow men any liberty, because, by their own nature, they tend in every instance to all kinds of degradation and demoralization.

We are therefore left to conjecture, in this case, upon what foundation universal suffrage is claimed for them with so much importunity.

The pretensions of organizers suggest another question, which I have often asked them, and to which I am not aware that I ever received an answer: Since the natural tendencies of mankind are so bad that it is not safe to allow them liberty, how comes it to pass that the tendencies of organizers are always good? Do not the legislators and their agents form a part of the human race? Do they consider that they are composed of different materials from the rest of mankind? They say that society, when left to itself, rushes to inevitable destruction, because its instincts are perverse. They presume to stop it in its downward course, and to give it a better direction. They have, therefore, received from heaven, intelligence and virtues that place them beyond and above mankind: let them show their title to this superiority. They would be our shepherds, and we are to be their flock. This arrangement presupposes in them a natural superiority, the right to which we are fully justified in calling upon them to prove.

You must observe that I am not contending against their right to invent social combinations, to propagate them, to recommend them, and to try them upon themselves, at their own expense and risk; but I do dispute their right to impose them upon us through the medium of the law, that is, by force and by public taxes.

I would not insist upon the Cabetists, the Fourierists, the Proudhonians, the Academics, and the Protectionists renouncing their own particular ideas; I would only have them renounce the idea that is common to them all—viz., that of subjecting us by force to their own categories and rankings to their social laboratories, to their ever-inflating bank, to their Greco-Roman morality, and to their commercial restrictions. I would ask them to allow us the faculty of judging of their plans, and not to oblige us to adopt them if we find that they hurt our interests or are repugnant to our consciences.

To presume to have recourse to power and taxation, besides being oppressive and unjust, implies further, the pernicious assumption that the organized is infallible, and mankind incompetent.

And if mankind is not competent to judge for itself, why do they talk so much about universal suffrage?

This contradiction in ideas is unhappily to be found also in facts; and whilst the French nation has preceded all others in obtaining its rights, or rather its political claims, this has by no means prevented it from being more governed, and directed, and imposed upon, and fettered, and cheated, than any other nation. It is also the one, of all others, where revolutions are constantly to be dreaded, and it is perfectly natural that it should be so.

So long as this idea is retained, which is admitted by all our politicians, and so energetically expressed by Mr. Louis Blanc in these words—"Society receives its impulse from power," so long as men consider themselves as capable of feeling, yet passive—incapable of raising themselves by their own discernment and by their own energy to any morality, or well-being, and while they expect everything from the law; in a word, while they admit that their relations with the State are the same as those of the flock with the shepherd, it is clear that the responsibility of power is immense. Fortune and misfortune, wealth and destitution, equality and inequality all proceed from it. It is charged with everything, it undertakes everything, it does everything; therefore it has to answer for everything. If we are happy, it has a right to claim our gratitude; but if we are miserable, it alone must bear the blame. Are not our persons and property in fact, at its disposal? Is not the law omnipotent? In creating the educational monopoly, it has undertaken to answer the expectations of fathers of families who have been deprived of liberty; and if these expectations are disappointed, whose fault is it?

In regulating industry, it has undertaken to make it prosper, otherwise it would have been absurd to deprive it of its liberty; and if it suffers, whose fault is it? In pretending to adjust the balance of commerce by the game of tariffs, it undertakes to make commerce prosper; and if, so far from prospering, it is destroyed, whose fault is it? In granting its protection to maritime armaments in exchange for their liberty, it has undertaken to render them self-sufficient; if they become burdensome, whose fault is it?

Thus, there is not a grievance in the nation for which the Government does not voluntarily make itself responsible. Is it any wonder that every failure threatens to cause a revolution? And what is the remedy proposed? To extend indefinitely the dominion of the law, i.e., the responsibility of Government. But if the Government undertakes to raise and to regulate wages, and is not able to do it; if it undertakes to assist all those who are in want, and is not able to do it; if it undertakes to provide work for every laborer, and is not able to do it; if it undertakes to offer to all who wish to borrow, easy credit, and is not able to do it; if, in words that we regret should have escaped the pen of Mr. de Lamartine, "the State considers that its mission is to enlighten, to develop, to enlarge, to strengthen, to spiritualize, and to sanctify the soul of the people"—if it fails in this, is it not obvious that after every disappointment, which, alas! is more than probable, there will be a no less inevitable revolution?

I shall now resume the subject by remarking, that immediately after the economical part[4] of the question, and before the political part, a leading question presents itself. It is the following:

What is law? What ought it to be? What is its domain? What are its limits? Where, in fact, does the prerogative of the legislator stop?

I have no hesitation in answering, Law is common force organized to prevent injustice;—in short, Law is Justice.

It is not true that the legislator has absolute power over our persons and property, since they pre-exist, and his work is only to secure them from injury.

It is not true that the mission of the law is to regulate our consciences, our ideas, our will, our education, our sentiments, our works, our exchanges, our gifts, our enjoyments. Its mission is to prevent the rights of one from interfering with those of another, in any one of these things.

Law, because it has force for its necessary sanction, can only have the domain of force, which is justice.

And as every individual has a right to have recourse to force only in cases of lawful defense, so collective force,

---

[4]Political economy precedes politics: the former has to discover whether human interests are harmonious or antagonistic, a fact which must be settled before the latter can determine the prerogatives of Government.

which is only the union of individual forces, cannot be rationally used for any other end.

The law, then, is solely the organization of individual rights that existed before law.

Law is justice.

So far from being able to oppress the people, or to plunder their property, even for a philanthropic end, its mission is to protect the people, and to secure to them the possession of their property.

It must not be said, either, that it may be philanthropic, so long as it abstains from all oppression; for this is a contradiction. The law cannot avoid acting upon our persons and property; if it does not secure them, then it violates them if it touches them.

The law is justice.

Nothing can be more clear and simple, more perfectly defined and bounded, or more visible to every eye; for justice is a given quantity, immutable and unchangeable, and which admits of neither increase or diminution.

Depart from this point, make the law religious, fraternal, equalizing, industrial, literary, or artistic, and you will be lost in vagueness and uncertainty; you will be upon unknown ground, in a forced Utopia, or, what is worse, in the midst of a multitude of contending Utopias, each striving to gain possession of the law, and to impose it upon you; for fraternity and philanthropy have no fixed limits, as justice has. Where will you stop? Where is the law to stop? One person, Mr. de Saint Cricq, will only extend his philanthropy to some of the industrial classes, and will require the law to slight the consumers in favor of the producers. Another, like Mr. Considerant, will take up the cause of the working classes, and claim for them by means of the law, at a fixed rate, clothing, lodging, food, and everything necessary for the support of life. A third, Mr. Louis Blanc, will say, and with reason, that this would be an incomplete fraternity, and that the law ought to provide them with tools of labor and education. A fourth will observe that such an arrangement still leaves room for inequality, and that the law ought to introduce into the most remote hamlets luxury, literature, and the arts. This is the high road to communism; in other words, legislation will be—as it now is—the battlefield for everybody's dreams and everybody's covetousness.

Law is justice.

In this proposition we represent to ourselves a simple, immovable Government. And I defy anyone to tell me whence the thought of a revolution, an insurrection, or a simple disturbance could arise against a public force confined to the repression of injustice. Under such a system, there would be more well-being, and this well-being would be more equally distributed; and as to the sufferings inseparable from humanity, no one would think of accusing the Government of them, for it would be as innocent of them as it is of the variations of the temperature. Have the people ever been known to rise against the court of appeals, or assail the justices of the peace, for the sake of claiming the rate of wages, free credit, tools of labor, the advantages of the tariff, or the social workshop? They know perfectly well that these matters are beyond the jurisdiction of the justices of the peace, and they would soon learn that they are not within the jurisdiction of the law quite as much.

But if the law were to be made upon the principle of fraternity, if it were to be proclaimed that from it proceed all benefits and all evils—that it is responsible for every individual grievance and for every social inequality—then you open the door to an endless succession of complaints, irritations, troubles, and revolutions.

Law is justice.

And it would be very strange if it could properly be anything else! Is not justice right? Are not rights equal? With what show of right can the law interfere to subject me to the social plans of Messrs. Mimerel, de Melun, Thiers, or Louis Blanc, rather than to subject these gentlemen to my plans? Is it to be supposed that Nature has not bestowed upon me sufficient imagination to invent a Utopia too? Is it for the law to make choice of one amongst so many fancies, and to make use of the public force in its service?

Law is justice.

And let it not be said, as it continually is, that the law, in this sense, would be atheistic, individual, and heartless, and that it would mold mankind in its own image. This is an absurd conclusion, quite worthy of the governmental infatuation which sees mankind in the law.

What then? Does it follow that if we are free, we shall cease to act? Does it follow that if we do not receive an impulse from the law, we shall receive no impulse at all? Does it follow that if the law confines itself to securing to us the free exercise of our faculties, our faculties will be paralyzed? Does it follow, that if the law does not impose upon us forms of religion, modes of association, methods of education, rules for labor, directions for exchange, and plans for charity, we shall plunge headlong into atheism, isolation, ignorance, misery, and greed? Does it follow, that we shall no longer recognize the power and goodness of God; that we shall cease to associate together, to help each other, to love and assist our unfortunate brethren, to study the secrets of nature, and to aspire after perfection in our existence?

Law is justice.

And it is under the law of justice, under the reign of right, under the influence of liberty, security, stability, and responsibility, that every man will attain to the fullness of his worth, to all the dignity of his being, and that mankind will accomplish with order and with calmness—slowly, it is true, but with certainty—the progress ordained for it.

I believe that my theory is correct; for whatever be the question upon which I am arguing, whether it be religious, philosophical, political, or economical; whether it affects well-being, morality, equality, right, justice, progress, responsibility, property, labor, exchange, capital, wages, taxes, population, credit, or Government; at whatever point of the scientific horizon I start from, I invariably come to the same thing—the solution of the social problem is in liberty.

And have I not experience on my side? Cast your eye over the globe. Which are the happiest, the most moral, and the most peaceable nations? Those where the law interferes the least with private activity; where the Government is the least felt; where individuality has the most scope, and public opinion the most influence; where the machinery of the administration is the least important and the least complicated; where taxation is lightest and least unequal, popular discontent the least excited and the least justifiable; where the responsibility of individuals and classes is the most active, and where, consequently, if morals are not in a perfect state, at any rate they tend incessantly to correct themselves; where transactions, meetings, and associations are the least fettered; where labor, capital, and production suffer the least from artificial displacements; where mankind follows most completely its own natural course; where the thought of God prevails the most over the inventions of men; those, in short, who realize the most nearly this idea that within the limits of right, all should flow from the free, perfectible, and voluntary action of man; nothing be attempted by the law or by force, except the administration of universal justice.

I cannot avoid coming to this conclusion—that there are too many great men in the world; there are too many legislators, organizers, institutors of society, conductors of the people, fathers of nations, etc., etc. Too many persons place themselves above mankind, to rule and patronize it; too many persons make a trade of looking after it. It will be answered—"You yourself are occupied upon it all this time." Very true. But it must be admitted that it is in another sense entirely that I am speaking; and if I join the reformers it is solely for the purpose of inducing them to relax their hold.

I am not doing as Vaucauson did with his automaton, but as a physiologist does with the human frame; I would study and admire it.

I am acting with regard to it in the spirit that animated a celebrated traveler. He found himself in the midst of a savage tribe. A child had just been born, and a crowd of soothsayers, magicians, and quacks were around it, armed with rings, hooks, and bandages. One said—"This child will never smell the perfume of a calumet, unless I stretch his nostrils." Another said—"He will be without the sense of hearing, unless I draw his ears down to his shoulders." A third said—"He will never see the light of the sun, unless I give his eyes an oblique direction." A fourth said—"He will never be upright, unless I bend his legs." A fifth said—"He will not be able to think, unless I press his brain." "Stop!" said the traveler. "Whatever God does, is well done; do not pretend to know more than He; and as He has given organs to this frail creature, allow those organs to develop themselves, to strengthen themselves by exercise, use, experience, and liberty."

God has implanted in mankind also all that is necessary to enable it to accomplish its destinies. There is a providential social physiology, as well as a providential human physiology. The social organs are constituted so as to enable them to develop harmoniously in the grand air of liberty. Away, then, with quacks and organizers! Away with their rings, and their chains, and their hooks, and their pincers! Away with their artificial methods! Away with their social laboratories, their governmental whims, their centralization, their tariffs, their universities, their State religions, their inflationary or monopolizing banks, their limitations, their restrictions, their moralizations, and their equalization by taxation! And now, after having vainly inflicted upon the social body so many systems, let them end where they ought to have begun—reject all systems, and try liberty—liberty, which is an act of faith in God and in His work.

Index